JUL   2013

D0903154

CM PUNK

BY TONY SMITH

BELLWETHER MEDIA · MINNEAPOLIS, MN

Are you ready to take it to the extreme?
Torque books thrust you into the action-packed world
of sports, vehicles, mystery, and adventure. These books
may include dirt, smoke, fire, and dangerous stunts.
WARNING : read at your own risk.

Library of Congress Cataloging-in-Publication Data

Smith, Tony.
 CM Punk / by Tony Smith.
    p. cm. -- (Torque: Pro wrestling champions)
 Includes bibliographical references and index.
 Summary: "Engaging images accompany information about CM Punk. The combination of high-interest subject matter and light text is intended for students in grades 3 through 7"--Provided by publisher.
 ISBN 978-1-60014-750-0 (hardcover : alk. paper)
 1. CM Punk, 1978---Juvenile literature. 2. Wrestlers--United States--Biography--Juvenile literature. I. Title.
 GV1196.C25S65 2012
 796.812092--dc23   2011036886

This edition first published in 2012 by Bellwether Media, Inc.

Printed in the United States of America, North Mankato, MN.

010112   1202

CONTENTS

MR. MONEY IN THE BANK

All eyes were on CM Punk as he entered the ring for the Money in the Bank match at WrestleMania 25. Fans called him "Mr. Money in the Bank" because he dominated this **ladder match**. CM Punk would battle seven other wrestlers for a briefcase hanging above the ring. The first man to climb a ladder and take it would be the winner.

QUICK HIT!

CM Punk trained in Muay Thai. This combat sport comes from Thailand. It combines parts of kickboxing and wrestling.

KANE

VITAL STATS

Wrestling Name: _____ CM Punk

Real Name: _____ Phillip Jack Brooks

Height: _____ 6 feet, 2 inches (1.9 meters)

Weight: _____ 218 pounds (99 kilograms)

Started Wrestling: _____ Mid-1990s

Finishing Move: _____ Go To Sleep (G.T.S.)

Only CM Punk and Kane were left standing after 15 minutes of fighting. Both men were climbing the ladder in the center of the ring. CM Punk stopped Kane just before he could grab the case. A kick to the head sent Kane flying down to the mat. CM Punk wasted no time. He reached the top and grabbed the case. He had won the match! CM Punk became the first wrestler to win the Money in the Bank two years in a row!

WHO IS CM PUNK?

Phillip Jack Brooks was born on October 26, 1978 in Chicago, Illinois. Phillip's father struggled with an **addiction** to alcohol. It was hard on Phillip and his family. In high school, Phillip discovered a punk rock band called Minor Threat. The band promoted a "straight edge" lifestyle without drugs, alcohol, or tobacco. Phillip **vowed** to be straight edge.

QUICK HIT!

CM Punk has many tattoos. One across his stomach reads "straight edge." Another on his left arm states "luck is for losers."

Phillip had an interest in combat sports. He was skilled in **karate** and **kickboxing**. He wrestled in the Lunatic Wrestling Federation (LWF) with his brother in the mid-1990s. The LWF was a **backyard wrestling** league. At one event, Phillip had to fill in for a member of the Chick Magnets tag team. His partner was called CM Venom. Phillip chose the name CM Punk.

CM Punk wanted to wrestle at the professional level. He went to a wrestling school called Steel Domain. By 2000, CM Punk was wrestling in several independent leagues. In 2005, World Wrestling Entertainment (WWE) offered CM Punk a **developmental contract**.

BECOMING A CHAMPION

QUICK HIT!

CM Punk gave himself the nickname "The Straight Edge Superstar."

CM Punk started his WWE career in Ohio Valley Wrestling (OVW). He became the OVW Champion in only two months. In June 2006, he moved to Extreme Championship Wrestling (ECW). He became a **face** there. He won the ECW Championship in 2007 and the World Heavyweight Championship in 2008.

CM Punk became a **heel** in 2009. He told fans and other wrestlers that they had to follow the straight edge lifestyle. He gave **sermons** and acted like he was the leader of a **cult**. This made him unpopular with fans. However, he remained a force in the ring. In 2011, he beat John Cena for the WWE Championship.

QUICK HIT!

CM Punk suffered a hip injury in November 2010. He couldn't wrestle for a few months. He became a WWE television announcer during that time.

DIVING
CROSSBODY

CM Punk uses a wide range of **signature moves**. One is the Anaconda Vise. He wraps his arm around the neck and one arm of his opponent. He holds the move until the opponent passes out. CM Punk also uses the Diving Crossbody. He jumps from the top rope and turns his body in midair. Then he slams into his opponent's chest and brings him to the mat.

Fans know the match is almost over when CM Punk performs a Go To Sleep (G.T.S.). Few opponents can withstand this powerful **finishing move**. CM Punk lifts his opponent into the air. Then he lifts his knee and drops the opponent. The opponent's face smashes into CM Punk's knee. It's usually lights out for the opponent and another victory for CM Punk.

GO TO SLEEP
(G.T.S.)

GLOSSARY

addiction—a physical or mental dependence on a substance such as a drug or alcohol

backyard wrestling—a form of amateur or semi-professional wrestling that takes place in very small venues, such as a person's backyard

cult—a small group of people who have beliefs that are seen by most as strange or evil

developmental contract—an agreement in which a wrestler signs with WWE but wrestles in a smaller league to gain experience and develop skills

face—a wrestler seen by fans as a hero

finishing move—a wrestling move meant to finish off an opponent so that he can be pinned

heel—a wrestler seen by fans as a villain

karate—a system of unarmed combat developed in Japan; karate is mostly used for self-defense.

kickboxing—a combat sport that combines boxing with martial arts

ladder match—a wrestling match in which a ladder is placed in the middle of the ring; the first wrestler to reach the object at the top wins the match.

sermons—speeches about moral subjects and behavior

signature moves—moves that a wrestler is famous for performing

vowed—promised

TO LEARN MORE

AT THE LIBRARY

Black, Jake. *The Ultimate Guide to WWE*. New York, N.Y.: Grosset & Dunlap, 2010.

Kaelberer, Angie Peterson. *Cool Pro Wrestling Facts*. Mankato, Minn.: Capstone Press, 2011.

Stone, Adam. *John Cena*. Minneapolis, Minn.: Bellwether Media, 2011.

ON THE WEB

Learning more about CM Punk is as easy as 1, 2, 3.

1. Go to www.factsurfer.com.

2. Enter "CM Punk" into the search box.

3. Click the "Surf" button and you will see a list of related Web sites.

With factsurfer.com, finding more information is just a click away.

INDEX